HOW TO BUILD YOUR OWN COUNTRY

Written by Valerie Wyatt
Illustrated by Karen Fredericks

A collection of books that inform children about the
world and inspire them to be engaged global citizens

KIDS CAN PRESS

For my wonderful aunt, Marie Anderson — V.W.

To my husband, Rick Murphy, without whom there would be no Glorious Empire of Rick & Karenistan, where I am fondly known as HRH, Princess Paininthebutt — K.F.

Acknowledgment

Writing a book is a solo endeavor, but publishing requires a group effort. I have been extremely fortunate to work on this book with the three Karens. Designer Karen Powers, as always, came up with an unusual and distinctive design that perfectly complements the text. Illustrator Karen Fredericks added the humor and brought Bathmatia to life. And editor Karen Li did what good editors do: moved the project forward, improving it at each stage and somehow managing to keep everyone engaged and happy. I am very grateful to them all.

First paperback edition 2024

CitizenKid™ is a trademark of Kids Can Press Ltd.

Text © 2009 Valerie Wyatt
Illustrations © 2009 Karen Fredericks

Information updated October 2023

Published in Canada and the U.S. by Kids Can Press Ltd.
25 Dockside Drive, Toronto, ON M5A 0B5

Kids Can Press is a Corus Entertainment Inc. company

www.kidscanpress.com

Edited by Karen Li
Designed by Karen Powers

Printed and bound in Malaysia in 10/2023 by Times Offset

CM 09 0 9 8 7
CM PA 24 0 9 8 7 6 5 4 3 2 1

FSC
www.fsc.org
MIX
Paper from responsible sources
FSC® C001507

Library and Archives Canada Cataloguing in Publication

Title: How to build your own country / written by Valerie Wyatt ; illustrated by Karen Fredericks.
Names: Wyatt, Valerie, author. | Fredericks, Karen, illustrator.
Series: CitizenKid.
Description: Series statement: CitizenKid | Includes index. | Previously published in 2009.
Identifiers: Canadiana 20230467717 | ISBN 9781554533114 (softcover)
Subjects: LCSH: Civics — Juvenile literature. | LCSH: Citizenship — Juvenile literature.
Classification: LCC JF801 .W93 2024 | DDC j320.4 — dc23

Kids Can Press gratefully acknowledges that the land on which our office is located is the traditional territory of many nations, including the Mississaugas of the Credit, the Anishnabeg, the Chippewa, the Haudenosaunee and the Wendat peoples, and is now home to many diverse First Nations, Inuit and Métis peoples.

We thank the Government of Ontario, through Ontario Creates and the Ontario Arts Council; the Canada Council for the Arts; and the Government of Canada for their financial support of our publishing activity.

Canada Council for the Arts   Conseil des arts du Canada

ONTARIO ARTS COUNCIL
CONSEIL DES ARTS DE L'ONTARIO
an Ontario government agency
un organisme du gouvernement de l'Ontario

Ontario

Contents

How to Build Your Own Country

Suppose you stumble across a chunk of land that no one owns. You could take it over and declare it a brand-new country. Your own personal country! The Kingdom of Jason! The Federal Republic of Katie! Even if it were only the size of a bath mat, it would be yours, all yours!

If you think that's highly unlikely, you're right. Unlikely, but not impossible. While 99.999999 percent of the planet is owned by one country or another, odd bits and pieces aren't, such as the abandoned World War II sea fortress that Roy Bates and his family took over in 1967 and declared the Principality of Sealand. A lot of people thought the island platform was owned by Britain, but the courts ruled it was in international waters and thus up for grabs. Today Sealand has its own flag, motto, national anthem and even postage stamps and coins. If Prince Roy of Sealand (as he is now called) can do it, so can you.

How exactly do you go about building a country from scratch? It's as easy as 1, 2, 3.

1 Stake out your identity … with a flag, money and a national anthem. In other words, put your country's brand name on the map.

2 Run the country … with a government, constitution, laws and an economy. Without these, your country will soon be one big unruly dilapidated mess.

3 Meet the neighbors … and join other nations on the big issues that face the whole world, such as poverty and climate change and security and international aid and …

Having Trouble Finding a Chunk of Land?

Don't despair. Many people who have wanted to build a country have had this problem. Here's how they've overcome it:

Assemble a country out of bits and pieces

A group of artists set up the Kingdom of Elgaland-Vargaland by claiming the land along the borders of the world's countries plus strips of ocean beyond their territorial waters. Sure, their micronation* is made of snippets scattered all over the globe, but it's still theirs. Or so they claim. Take a tip from them and look for scraps of land that aren't clearly owned by anyone.

Get out your magnifying glass

All around the world are tiny parcels of land that no one has ever bothered with. Some are islands that have recently surfaced in the oceans. In 1997, Gregory Green laid claim to a teensy coral isle poking up in the South Pacific for the New Free State of Caroline. Unfortunately, a mere two years later, the nearby country of Kiribati took the island for itself.

Nothing succeeds like secession

Secession (breaking away from an existing country) is a surefire way to start a new country. The Republic of Molossia (population: thirty) is a micronation Kevin Baugh formed by breaking away from the state of Nevada. So far, the United Nations has not recognized Molossia as an independent country.

Go virtual

Who says you need land to have a country? Several countries exist only on the Internet. Lizbekistan, for example, was an e-country that lasted for three glorious years until its founder, Liz Stirling, shut it down in 1999. Lizbekistan once had several thousand e-citizens.

* **Mi-cro-na-tion**
(my-kro'-nay'-shun) n.
A country that someone has made up and that is not recognized by real countries.

STEP #1:
Stake Out Your Identity

If you're going to start a country, you've got to let the world know you exist. Why? Because having a public profile will help you attract a population and maybe even tourists. A name, a flag, a national anthem and a motto shout, "Hey, we're here!"

They can also be used to say something about your country. Bathmatia, for example, may only be the size of a large bath mat, but its flag (and national haircut) say it's a very clean and orderly nation.

Welcome to BATHMATIA

Naming Your Country

There are really no rules you have to follow here. Country names can be descriptive (Iceland), colorful (Greenland) or directional (South Africa). Or they can say something about who's in charge (Kingdom of Sweden; People's Republic of China). They can be simple (Togo) or fancy (Most Serene Republic of San Marino).

Most Serene Empire of **Lazyland**

Want to name your country after yourself? To be honest, this doesn't happen all that often in the real world. Simón Bolívar was one of the few people who had this honor. Bolivia was named after him in 1825 because he led its struggle for independence from Spain. But if you insist ... just chop off the last bit of your name (first or last) and add "a" or "ia."

Another popular option is to tack on "land" or "stan," as in Kyrgyzstan, Kazakhstan, Uzbekistan and Tajikistan. ("Stan" means "land" in several languages.) This may not work if your name is Stan.

United Federation of **Pinkistan**

Some countries choose a name that says something about their citizens. The "turk" in Turkey and Turkmenistan means "strong." Why not go with something like Bravestan or Lazyland or Popularia?

Just one warning: You'll need to work your country's name into a national anthem (page 14), so you might want to make it something hum-able. We are pretty sure the folks in Equatorial Guinea didn't think this through.

The Republic of **Marge and Tina**

U-Name-It

If you get really stuck and can't seem to settle on the perfect name for your country, use this handy chart to help you pick one. Choose the first half from Column A, and then pick a fitting description from Column B. Presto! You've got yourself a name.

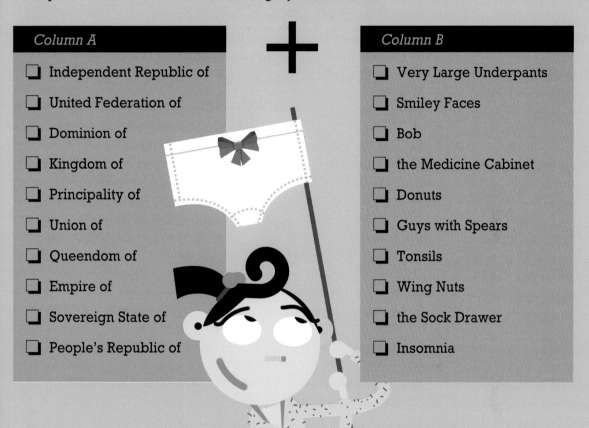

Column A + **Column B**

Column A	Column B
☐ Independent Republic of	☐ Very Large Underpants
☐ United Federation of	☐ Smiley Faces
☐ Dominion of	☐ Bob
☐ Kingdom of	☐ the Medicine Cabinet
☐ Principality of	☐ Donuts
☐ Union of	☐ Guys with Spears
☐ Queendom of	☐ Tonsils
☐ Empire of	☐ Wing Nuts
☐ Sovereign State of	☐ the Sock Drawer
☐ People's Republic of	☐ Insomnia

Name Changes

Don't worry if you use your name for a while and decide you don't particularly like it. No problem. Many countries change names, sometimes several times. Today's Iran was known as Persia until 1935. Ceylon was renamed Sri Lanka in 1972. Upper Volta became Burkina Faso in 1984. (No wonder they changed — who would want to be called an Upper Voltan?) But, for the most part, countries tend to hang onto their names, only renaming themselves if there's been a revolution or other big change in power.

Imastan
Whomea
Awesomnia

9

No one says you need to have a huge population, especially if your country is only the size of a bath mat. But you'll need some sort of population, because without citizens your country will be … well, just another bath mat.

Start by asking friends and family members to move to your country. If they won't cooperate, here are some other possibilities:

Attract immigrants

These are people from other countries who might be willing to move to your country in search of a better life. In the early 1900s, for example, Canada offered free farmland to immigrants.

Conquer a neighboring country

Conquering is definitely a risky business, as nations all through history have discovered. Most countries don't want to be invaded, so doing it requires a lot of force. And beware: They may not stay conquered forever. Mexico was captured by Spain in 1519, but then threw out its rulers and declared independence in 1810.

Annex a neighboring country

This is a more peaceful and sometimes legal variation of conquering. It means that you take over a country and make it part of your own. Like conquered countries, annexed countries may not be happy about giving up their independence. East Timor was annexed by Indonesia in 1975, but the East Timorese fought for independence, which they regained in 2002. Their country is now called the Democratic Republic of Timor-Leste.

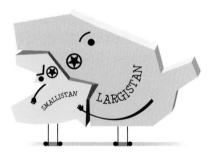

Welcome refugees

People who are forced to flee their homeland because they are in danger may be eager to move to your country. Vietnamese boat people — refugees who fled their country by boat after the Vietnam War — were welcomed by many nations, including the United States, Australia, Canada and France.

Passports

The first passports were simply handwritten notes signed by a king or queen requesting safe passage for the bearer. Today's passports are just a fancy version of those notes — with lots of extra security features to keep criminals from stealing and using them.

If your citizens want to travel, they too will want passports. You can make them out of small notebooks or folded pieces of paper.

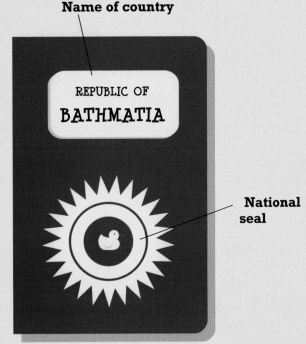

Name of country

REPUBLIC OF
BATHMATIA

National seal

Photo of citizen

Passport number

82619821988878993324330b5222

Jan. 1, 2024

Dec. 31, 2034

Dates of issue and expiry

34662-77732

Nov. 14, 2016

Date of birth

Lintallova

Bathmatia

Place of birth

Name — Pasme DaSoapa

Nationality — Bathmatian

Sex — M

32433068261988882197899935222

Signature

Bunch of fancy numbers to thwart counterfeiters

Designing a Flag and Choosing a Motto

You want your flag to be big, bold and beautiful, so that as it waves in the wind over your capital city (if you have one) or is carried by your army (if you have one), it will bring tears to the eyes.

To make your flag world class, try some designs used by other nations, and then add a few personal touches.

1 Pick a background. Here are some basic ones to choose from. Combine two if you wish, but remember the number one rule of flag design: Keep it simple.

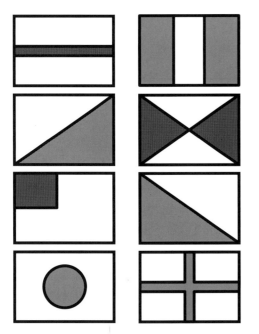

2 Add a decorative motif, such as a star, crest, leaf or animal. Or get a bit more personal and add something that screams YOU! (A TV remote, or maybe a skateboard?)

3 Pick your colors, and you're done.

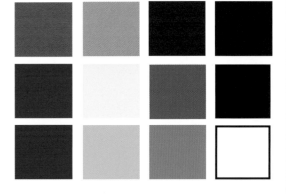

Your National Motto

Three little words. That's all many nations use for their national motto (a phrase or saying that sums up the hopes and dreams of a nation). Sometimes, it's the same three little words. The African countries of Burundi and Chad, for example, both have the motto "UNITY, WORK, PROGRESS."

If you'd prefer something a bit more original, why not go where no country has ever gone before? Pick three from among these words: lazy, divided, queasy, nitpicking, backward, grumpy, greedy, bored. We guarantee they've never been used in a national motto and probably never will be.

But don't feel limited by a three-word motto. Botswana, for example, chose a single word, "Pula" (Rain), which says a lot about what its people most hope for. Luxembourg has a whole sentence: "We want to remain what we are." Short or long, your motto is a chance to tell other countries what's important to *your* country.

BATHMATIA: Free and Glorious Lint

Writing a National Anthem

If you like to sing or can play an instrument, you're ahead of the game here. If not, don't worry — you can always "borrow" a national anthem from some small, helpless country that doesn't have an army to come after you.

Some things to keep in mind when composing an anthem:

● Instruments with big sounds, such as drums and trumpets, give any piece of music *oomph* and are great for national anthems.

● Be sure to sing your anthem out loud before formally adopting it. Better still, imagine 20 000 fans at a baseball game singing it. Because that's the thing about anthems — they are meant to be belted out, and not all of those belters will have good voices.

● Make it patriotic. Including some of the following words will help: glory, freedom, victory, honor, courage, motherland, homeland, strong, true.

● Pick a catchy tune. Here are some you might consider adapting: "Home on the Range," "Walking on Sunshine," "Do Your Ears Hang Low."

A Fill-in-the-Blanks National Anthem
(Sung to the tune of "Old MacDonald Had a Farm")

Hail _____ , _____ and true. We stand tall for you!
           name of country   *adjective*

A micronation that's brand new. Home to just a few.

With some _____ here and some _____ there.
                 plural noun   *plural noun*

Here a _____, there a _____, everywhere a _____ _____.
       noun   *noun*   *adjective*   *noun*

Hail _____ , _____ and true.
           name of country   *adjective*

We _____ and _____ for you!
       verb   *verb*

STEP #2:
Run the Country

Running a country is a bit like having pet fish. You have to take care of the fish or bad things will happen (to the fish). Actually, looking after a population is a lot more work than that because your citizens won't be satisfied with just food and clean water. They will expect big things, such as a justice system, a government and an economy, and smaller things, such as roads, schools and hospitals. These are the necessities that will help them lead healthy and prosperous lives. And if your citizens are healthy and prosperous, your country will be, too.

You may be saying to yourself, Why do I need a government? I can run the country myself! A government led by one person (queen, king, dictator) is called an autocracy. Having all the power may sound tempting, but history warns us that there are perils to being the sole ruler of a country, such as being deposed, overthrown or even decapitated. Instead, we suggest giving these other forms of government a shot.

A An **oligarchy**, in which the country is controlled by a family or a small group of aristocrats (as in Saudi Arabia).

B A **theocracy**, in which the government is run by religious leaders according to religious beliefs (as in Iran).

C A **single-party** government, in which one large group rules (as in China).

D A **democracy**, in which the people elect representatives to make decisions and govern (as in the United States, Canada, the United Kingdom and India).

And the winner is ...

Most countries either choose or would like to choose option D. Democracies put power in the hands of citizens. In fact, the word democracy comes from the Greek *demos*, which means "common people," and *kratos*, which means "rule" or "strength."

Democracies aren't perfect, but they tend to be freer and fairer than other systems of government because citizens have more control over the things that affect them. But don't take our word for it. Try out some of the other forms of government and see how your citizens like them. Just don't come crying to us if they behead you.

A Bad Example

Whatever you do, please don't follow the lead of Saparmurat Niyazov, the sole ruler of Turkmenistan from 1991 until his death in 2006. He was called "one of the wealthiest and most powerful lunatics on Earth," which might have been okay, except that he exerted his lunatic power over the five million or so citizens of Turkmenistan.

While Niyazov didn't seem to have much time to educate his people or create jobs (more than 60 percent of the population was unemployed under his rule), he did have time to ban ballet, opera, beards, the internet and listening to car radios. He also renamed the days of the week and months of the year (he named January after himself and April after his mother). But perhaps the most important work of this dictator was to erect hundreds of gold statues of himself. After all, if he didn't proclaim his magnificence, who would? Certainly not the people of Turkmenistan.

Holding Elections

If you picked option A, B or C on page 16, you don't need to read this section. There probably won't be any elections in your country. Elections only happen when citizens need to make decisions about their country, and that only happens in democracies. In other forms of government, citizens don't make the decisions; the decisions are made for them.

Say you chose option D — democracy. You could ask your citizens to vote on every issue that comes up, but you'd get awfully tired of counting votes. Other democratic countries have solved this problem with something called representative government. In a representative government, citizens vote for people who will represent them. These representatives debate issues on behalf of the people they represent and come to

decisions to benefit the whole country. Thousands of citizens might elect just one representative, so you end up with a smallish group of decision-makers — and a lot less vote counting.

Elections are about choosing representatives, but there's more to them than just that. To get votes, would-be representatives, called candidates, announce a set of ideas they say will guide them when making decisions if they are elected. They often join together with other people who share the same ideas to form a political party. So a vote for a candidate who belongs to a party is also a vote for that party's guiding principles.

It's a Fake!

Some countries hold elections to make themselves appear democratic, even though they're not. And they try to look more democratic by forming councils and assemblies, but these bodies don't have the power to make decisions. Why bother? The reputation of democracy is so high that even non-democratic countries try to seem democratic.

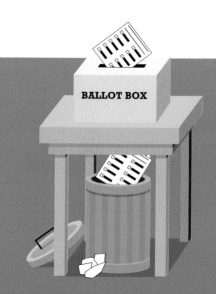

BALLOT BOX

The actual election process is pretty simple.

1 Citizens go to a voting place, show ID and get checked off a list of registered voters. This reduces voter fraud.

2 Voters mark a ballot (list of candidates) with their choice or choices. In most countries, it is a secret ballot — the voters mark it in secret to keep their choices private.

3 The ballots are counted. The candidates with the most votes get elected.

One Dog, One Vote

Duncan M. MacDonald cast his vote in a 2006 election in the United States. There was only one problem: Duncan was a dog. He was registered as a voter over the phone by his owner and was sent a mail-in ballot. (Mail-in ballots are used by voters who can't vote in person at election time.) Duncan marked his choice with a paw print, and then his owner, Jane Balogh, mailed in the ballot. Ms. Balogh was trying to make the point that it's too easy to get registered to vote because she was concerned about voter fraud. By registering Duncan to vote, she actually committed voter fraud. For doing so, she was convicted of making a false statement to a public official.

Your voters will want to know that the elections you hold are fair. They won't put up with dogs voting or people cheating by, say, using fake ID to vote more than once. After all, votes are precious. Voters only get one per election, and they want to use their vote to elect candidates who will best represent their values.

Fair elections also mean that everyone who wants to vote can. Imagine trying to vote only to find the nearest voting place was on an island, so that only swimmers could vote. Or imagine trying to vote and being asked for fourteen pieces of ID, including your great grandmother's birth certificate. You might just give up.

The citizens of your country want fair elections because they want their votes to be counted and to count.

Constitution

So your citizens have elected a bunch of representatives, and they're all milling around wanting staplers and pencils and parking spots. Why not put them to work governing the country? After all, it's what they were elected to do.

One great warm-up exercise is to write a constitution. Not all countries have constitutions, but they can be very handy. A constitution can set out the principles of a country and the rights of its citizens. It can also establish the various parts of the government, what each is responsible for and how they will share power.

A constitution also acts like the highest law of the country and puts limits on what other laws can do. So, for example, if your constitution says people in your country have the right to own goldfish, and then a law is passed outlawing goldfish, the constitution will overturn the law and you'll get to keep your goldfish. This also applies to more serious issues, such as freedom of speech and religion.

Your constitution should include:

(1) the principles of the country

(2) a statement about individual citizen's rights

(3) the role of the constitution as the top law

(4) the parts of the government

(5) how the parts work together

(6) a way to change the constitution in the future

> Why all the branches? It divides up the power, so that no one group has too much. Democracies work best when power is shared.

Constitution
of THE INDEPENDENT REPUBLIC of
Bathmatia

1   We the people declare that Bathmatia is founded on the principle of the rule of law and the rights of the individual.

2   We believe the individual has certain rights, foremost among them the right to life, freedom from discrimination, personal security and the right to own goldfish.

3   To ensure that the laws of the land support the rule of law and individuals' rights, we proclaim this constitution the supreme law of the land.

4   WHO DOES WHAT

We declare that the government of Bathmatia be divided into three branches:

Legislative
(the elected representatives who make the laws)

Executive
(the top elected official and his or her advisors who put the laws into effect)

Judicial
(the system of courts that enforces laws and resolves disputes)

5   These three branches shall have separate responsibilities and powers.

6   Changing this constitution will require the approval of two-thirds of the citizens of Bathmatia.

Laws are a bit like the rules of a game. But are they really necessary? Well, just imagine a soccer game without rules. Want extra players on the field? Go for it! A little tripping or shoving? No problem! Now imagine a whole country without rules. So, yes, your country will need laws.

Any country can make up a law — as long as it can be enforced. Let's say you don't like straight hair. Simply announce a law that bans it, and then enforce it by arresting and imprisoning all people with straight hair. Done!

On second thought … if your citizens are like the people of other countries, they will not obey laws that they feel are unjust or unequal, like imprisoning people just because they have straight hair or because they criticize the government or practice a certain religion.

The laws they *will* obey are laws that protect them, their freedoms and their property, and those that protect shared things, such as the environment. So keep that in mind when you're drafting laws.

Better yet, turn over the job of law-making to the people's representatives. The citizens have elected them to represent their interests. So they are more likely to obey laws that have been passed by those representatives, rather than ones that you've made up. That's another reason democracies are successful.

Spot the Fake Law

Eight of these are actual laws that once existed or continue to exist in parts of the world. But one is a fake. Can you guess which? Answers on page 39.

1. **Thailand:** *It is illegal to leave your house if you are not wearing underwear.*

2. **Italy:** *A man may be arrested for wearing a skirt.*

3. **Australia:** *It is illegal to feed a kangaroo in a restaurant.*

4. **Israel:** *It is forbidden to bring bears to the beach.*

5. **Denmark:** *No one may start a car while someone is underneath the vehicle.*

6. **Alabama:** *It is illegal for a driver to be blindfolded while operating a vehicle.*

7. **Canada:** *Citizens may not publicly remove bandages.*

8. **Alaska:** *It is illegal to push a live moose out of a moving airplane.*

9. **Pennsylvania:** *It is illegal to sleep on top of a refrigerator outdoors.*

Take It to Court

Most countries have a court system that's like a pyramid. At the bottom are the courts that judge the cases first. If one side doesn't think the judgment is fair, it can appeal to a higher court. At the top of the pyramid is the highest court in the country, sometimes called the high, supreme or constitutional court. This top-level court has the final say on who's guilty and who's innocent. Usually, it can also throw out laws that go against the principles set out in the country's constitution.

Running a country is a bit like running a business. Your customers are your citizens. Here are some of the things on their shopping list. The more things you can deliver, the happier your citizens will be.

- ❑ a clean environment
- ❑ jobs
- ❑ health care
- ❑ education
- ❑ defense (army, navy, air force)
- ❑ government services (postal system, passports, housing assistance)
- ❑ income assistance for the poor or elderly
- ❑ a justice system
- ❑ infrastructure (bridges, highways, ferries, airports, communication satellites, etc.)
- ❑ trade within the country and with other countries
- ❑ relations with other countries

The good news is that your citizens are willing (sort of) to pay for these things through taxes. BUT (and as you can see, it's a big "but") citizens want their tax money spent to keep the country running smoothly. If they think you are throwing money around on useless stuff or not spending money where it's needed, they will turf you next time there's an election.

You've got some choices about how to raise taxes. You can tax stuff (sales tax, property tax, import tax, etc.), so the more stuff people buy or own, the more tax they pay. Or you can tax earnings (incomes, inheritances, investments, etc.). If you want, you can tax stuff *and* earnings.

Whatever you decide, just remember tax money is not your money. It belongs to the people, so spend it wisely.

PAY TAXES AT
THE REGISTER

No-Tax Zone

Does the whole tax thing sound like a hassle? If so, make your country a tax haven, a place where citizens are not taxed or are taxed very little. More than twenty-five countries around the world are tax havens. They hope to attract individuals and businesses who want to dodge taxes in their home countries. They figure the tax dodgers' spending will make up for the lack of tax income. But beware: Tax havens aren't very popular with countries that do tax. They say tax havens reduce the amount of tax income paid to them.

Money

Did you notice that jobs were high on the shopping list on page 24? People need to earn money to support themselves and their families. And you can help them do this by making sure your country has an economy.

What exactly is an economy? It's the production, distribution, exchange and consumption of goods and services. Whew! Long ago, people didn't need an economy. They were self-sufficient — they hunted and grew and built and spun everything they needed. But once they started trading ("I'll give you a sack of wheat for that pig") — *voilà* — an instant economy. And the more specialized people became (in raising pigs, growing wheat, selling cars, making radios, designing websites), the bigger the economy grew.

Going Global or Staying Local?

Today, most countries' economies are linked with one another through trade and investment. Some people say too linked. They think that globalization ends up giving too much wealth to a few big corporations and too little money to poor countries and their workers. But if you decide not to trade with other countries, you may find that your country's economy doesn't grow and your citizens don't prosper. It's a balancing act.

You can choose to let the government run the economy. Several countries have attempted this. The former Soviet Union (now split into Russia and several other countries) had a government-run economy from 1917–1991. During this time, the government used the people's taxes to fund some brilliant successes, such as their space program. But they never managed to set up a healthy economy. Instead, they tried to tightly control all businesses, from butcher shops and clothing stores to factories and farms. Life became miserable for ordinary people, who were plagued by shortages of food, fuel and housing. Eventually, even the government had to admit they weren't doing such a great job. They let in private businesses to help fill the gaps.

You can go the other extreme by choosing to keep the government out of the economy. The fewer laws a government passes to control the economy, the more freedom businesses have to do what they want. The Vikings, for example, didn't have a lot of government control over their trading (or should we say raiding). Their plundering and pillaging in the ninth century may have made them rich, but it didn't exactly make them popular.

If your citizens are like the citizens of other countries, they'll probably prefer a mixed economy, with some rules from government and some freedom for businesses. Whatever you choose, keep in mind that your job is to keep the economy running smoothly so that your citizens prosper.

Cold, Hard Cash

Everyone likes to make money, but in your case, you'll be doing it literally. You'll need currency (coins and bills) that people can use for transactions in your country. Many countries put their kings and queens or other famous people on their money. But since this is your country, feel free to use your own likeness. And your currency should have a name. Warning: "dollar" has been taken by more than twenty countries, and "dinar" is also popular. If you want to stick with d-words, what about the "doo-dad" or the "dimple"?

Once you've named and manufactured currency, it's time to establish its value, and that will depend on how well your economy does. If your economy slumps, so will your dimple. If your economy booms, your dimple will, too.

Taking a
Holiday

You've been working hard on your country, and you're almost ready to join the other nations of the world. Before you do, why not take a break? Yes, you need a holiday, and so does your new country. You could all go to Disneyland, but depending on how many citizens you have, that could get expensive. Why not just party at home?

Many nations have holidays to celebrate events such as the day they were founded or became independent. Other holidays honor important individuals (America's Martin Luther King Jr. Day, India's Gandhi Jayanti). But if you're like us, you probably want to slip in a few more holidays. A good bet is a children's day — many countries have one of these. On Turkey's Children's Day (April 23), kids take over the Grand National Assembly and run the country for the day.

Or you could follow the lead of the Aerican Empire, a micronation started by five-year-old Eric Lis in Montreal in 1987 and still going strong. It has a whopping twenty-eight holidays, including October 12, International Moment of Frustration Scream Day, when citizens of the Empire are encouraged to go outside at noon and scream themselves silly.

STEP #3:
Meet the Neighbors

There are 195 countries in the world (not counting your new one) and many smaller territories, dependencies, colonies and other not-quite-countries. They're your neighbors, and you should get to know them. Why? Because no country is an island ... er ... except island countries.

We're all part of one big world, and sometimes we need to work together on issues like peace and climate change and disaster relief. So reach out a hand and introduce yourself. It's time to meet the neighbors.

Like all neighbors, the countries of the world are a mixed bunch. Some will be very like your country. Others will be very different.

In fact, countries, like people, come in a wide variety of shapes, sizes and "personalities."

Big and Small

The world's largest country is Russia, which is 17 075 200 square km (6 591 027 square mi.). The country with the biggest population is India, with around 1 429 000 000 people. Vatican City, in Rome, is the smallest country, with just 0.44 square km (0.27 square mi.), and it has the smallest population, around 800 people.

New and Old

One of the world's newest countries is South Sudan, which declared independence in 2011. The oldest country is San Marino, founded by a stonemason named Marino in the year 301. Good thing his name wasn't Bob.

Rich and Poor

Luxembourg wins the prize for the richest country in the world, while Burundi is the poorest. If you take the entire economy of a country and divide it by the number of people, you get something called the Gross Domestic Product (GDP) per capita. It's an indicator of the wealth — or poverty — of the country. Luxembourg's GDP per capita is $130 000 USD, while Burundi's GDP per capita is only $250 USD.

Crowded and Empty

Tiny Monaco has the most people per square kilometer — 18 215. Namibia has only three people per square kilometer.

Coming and Going

Thirty-three countries have come into existence since 1990, and others have vanished from the map, becoming part of other nations. But one country, Tuvalu in the South Pacific, is literally vanishing. The nine low-lying atolls (coral islands) that make up Tuvalu are at risk from rising sea levels caused by global warming. At current rates, the island nation may disappear beneath the waves some time in the next fifty years, and its 12 000 people will become environmental refugees in need of a new home.

A Tale of Two Yugoslavias

When the Central European country of Yugoslavia broke apart in the early 1990s, its name disappeared from maps of the world. But it seems not all Yugoslavians were willing to give up on their former country. Cyber Yugoslavia, an online micronation, started up in 1999 and claimed close to 17 000 e-citizens. Its citizens were from all over the world. They liked the idea of joining a place where everyone had to become a secretary (a kind of government minister) of something or other. There was the Secretary for Sunset, the Secretary for Ducks, the Secretary for Swimming and so on.

The founder of the country, Zoran Bacic, planned on applying to the United Nations for membership when the population of Cyber Yugoslavia hit five million. Sadly, Cyber Yugoslavia never reached this population and is no longer in existence today.

Joining the Club

Your country may not speak the same language as the neighbors or share their taste in food or national costume. But it's still worth joining with them to deal with issues that affect the whole neighborhood or even the whole world. Maybe you want to clean up a river that crosses several borders. Maybe one of the neighbors is bullying another, disturbing the peace. Maybe you'd like to join together to buy or sell things more easily. If so, form a club of countries that share your goals, preferably one that sounds good when turned into an acronym.

Take NATO, for example. It's the acronym for the North Atlantic Treaty Organization, a military group of thirty-one North American and European countries that focuses on security. Or there's ECOWAS, the Economic Community of West African States, a group of fifteen nations that promotes economic development. Start with a fun acronym (HOHO? SNORT? WINK?) and work backward to choose a name. (SNORT = Sovereign Nations of Rotting Tomatoes, an organization of tomato-growing countries that often find they have a few too many.)

The biggest of all the clubs in the world has a very small acronym: UN (United Nations). It's the closest thing we have to a world government. It doesn't have the authority to make laws and enforce them, but it does have all the countries of the world as its members. If one of them steps out of line by, say, killing part of its population, the other members can put pressure on that country to get it to stop.

The UN can also send in peacekeeping forces if conflicts break out.

Besides peacekeeping and other matters of international security, the UN tackles such issues as economic and social development, international law, human rights and relief for refugees of war or disaster. It's the number one club on the planet and definitely worth joining.

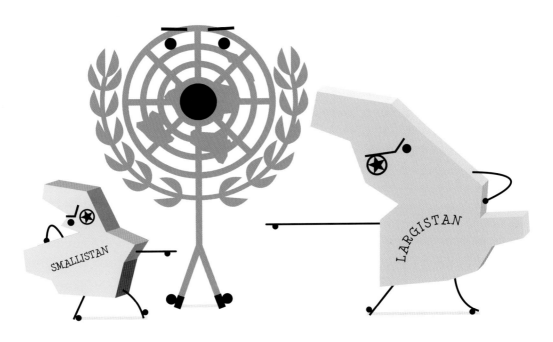

Getting Recognized

It's one thing to say you're a country, but another to have other countries accept you as one. Lots of would-be countries are striving for the r-word: recognition. Being recognized means you have diplomatic relations with other countries and better hopes of trade with them, as well as a greater chance of being accepted into the UN. How do you get your country recognized? It helps to have a permanent population, a form of government and a territory. That's a good start, but you'll still need to persuade other countries that you're a real country. Good luck!

Keeping the Peace

It's not enough to know the neighbors — you need to get along with them, even if you don't particularly like them. They may do things that irritate you, such as boasting and bragging or treating their citizens poorly; nonetheless, we all share one planet, so try to keep your cool.

But let's say your neighbor country is a real bully and does something that really bugs you, such as threatening to build nuclear weapons or claiming a corner of your country as its own. Do you roll out the cannons and let them have it?

Not just yet. Before you bring out the big guns, you have another weapon called diplomacy. You can send your ambassador to talk sense to the bully country's head of government. (An ambassador is a person who represents the interests of his or her country in another country.) Or maybe you can persuade the bully to sign a treaty

(agreement) with you to end the problem. You can also have an arbitrator (an impartial person) settle the matter or take it to an international court.

If talking fails, try announcing sanctions, such as refusing to trade or communicate with the bully. Cutting off a country's supply of chocolate or oil or rubber may make them smarten up.

If diplomacy fails, you may have to bring out the cannons, but this should be a last resort. Unless there is a really, really good reason for going to war, such as being invaded, your citizens are not going to approve of the killing and the expense. They're especially not going to be keen on sending troops to another country. Other countries may see you as an invader, which can be just as bad as being a bully. Better to ask for help from others, preferably through the UN, which can send in peacekeepers.

Hans Off

Hans Island, a small rocky island about 1100 km (680 mi.) south of the North Pole, is remote, isolated and unpopulated. But to Canada and Denmark, it's a very desirable chunk of land. It lies in the Northwest Passage, which may become an important northern shipping route between the Atlantic and Pacific oceans as ice coverage in the area decreases. Both countries want access to the route and the islands that dot it. So Canada and Denmark, usually good friends, have been scuffling over the island for years. One country erects a flagpole and hoists up its flag. Then the other takes down the flag and replaces it with its own. Soldiers from both sides have visited the island (at different times), as have government officials. Foreign ministers tried diplomacy. They met to discuss who owns Hans, but came to no agreement. Then, in July 2007, Canadian officials examined satellite images and put the boundary between Canada and Denmark right down the middle of the island, giving both countries a piece of Hans not much bigger than … well … a bath mat.

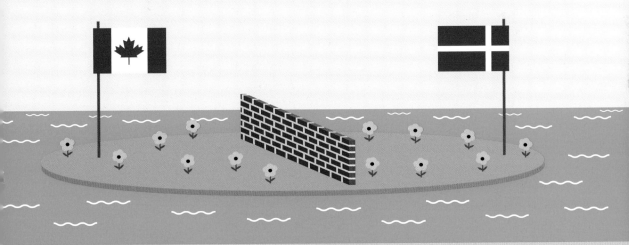

Blue Berets

Suppose civil war broke out in Bathmatia, with the tall people battling the short ones. You need to call in the Blue Berets — United Nations peacekeepers. (They wear blue berets to make sure everyone knows they're from the UN.) UN peacekeepers get sent into all kinds of conflict zones, from civil wars to clashes over borders and more. They are not the UN's own soldiers, but rather soldiers from UN-member countries who believe that peace is preferable to war.

Put It All Together and You Get ...

... your very own brand-spanking-new country, ready to take its place in the world.

Does starting and running a country sound like pure fantasy to you?

Not to Bobby Madison, who founded the micronation of Talossa in 1979, when he was fourteen. It was located in his bedroom — actually, it *was* his bedroom — in Milwaukee, Wisconsin. (*Talossa* is Finnish for "inside the house.") He had to cross the border into the United States every time he went to the bathroom.

Bobby (now King Robert) convinced friends to become citizens, set up a government and laws, and even created an extensive written language of 28 000 words. (*Dïeu t'alegra* means "Have a nice day!") The country also claims an island off France and a chunk of Antarctica.

Talossa continues to this day, but after a power struggle between King Robert and Talossan citizens, it has recently split into the Kingdom of Talossa and the Republic of Talossa (run by citizens, not a king). Like real-world countries, Talossa changes over time.

THE KINGDOM OF TALOSSA

KEEP OUT!

Child Rulers

There hasn't yet been a child who has started a real country, but there have been lots of young people who have ruled their countries. Emperor Puyi of China came to the throne in 1908, at the ripe old age of two. And Mary Stuart became Queen of Scotland when she was just six days old. Puyi and Mary were not alone. Many other countries have also had young rulers.

So, yes, you can build a country, even if it's just among friends or on the internet. One thing to remember, though: Be good to your people. They're your greatest asset. If you are mean or unfair to your citizens or ignore their wishes, you may find yourself in the middle of a revolution and that could be downright painful. To you. (Remember? Page 17? Beheading?)

Good luck with your country. And if you're ever in the area, please come and visit Bathmatia. We're just south of the sink, off the coast of the bathtub. We'd love to show you around and send you home with a lifetime supply of lint.

Bathmatia Fact File

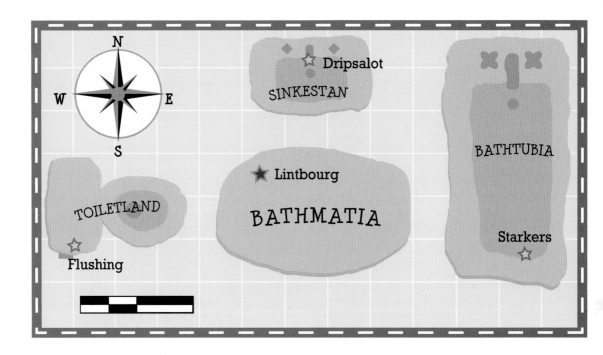

Status: Democracy

Area: 0.000000000000001 square km (0.000000000000001 square mi.)

Capital city: Lintbourg

Population: Three (including dog)

Languages: English, Bathmatian

Currency: The Fuzz

Gross Domestic Product: ℱ 48 212 per person (except the dog)

Motto: Free and Glorious Lint

Flag:

National day: Come Clean Day, June

Main products: Lint

Main exports: Lint, happiness

Glossary

citizens: the people who live in a country and who have rights and responsibilities in that country

constitution: the highest law in a country. Also often describes how the parts of government will share power.

democracy: a system of government in which the people hold the power in a country, usually through representatives they elect

economy: a system of producing, distributing, trading and consuming goods (such as food) and services (such as nursing)

elections: a process in which citizens vote for representatives who will make decisions about the country on their behalf

globalization: the interaction of governments and private companies around the world in areas such as trade, technology and investment

government: the body of representatives, laws and policies that run a country

micronation: a small and sometimes made-up country not recognized by other countries

political party: a group of people who share certain beliefs and policies. Some countries have only one party (like China) but most countries have two or more competing parties.

refugees: people who leave, or who are forced out of, their country, usually for safety or economic reasons

secession: when one part of a country leaves the rest of a country

taxes: money paid by citizens to the government to take care of roads, schools, bridges, the military, the environment and other shared public property and institutions

voting: casting a ballot for a person who seeks to serve as a representative in government

nswer to the quiz on page 23:
e fake law is #3. All the rest really have been laws at one time or other in their
untry or state.

Index